No Redneck Left Behind

Facing the Real World
After Gettin' Your Diploma

Jeff Foxworthy

With illustrations by David Boyd

RUTLEDGE HILL PRESS

Nashville, Tennessee

A Division of Thomas Nelson Publishers

Since 1798

www.thomasnelson.com

Published by Rutledge Hill Press, a Division of Thomas Nelson, Inc., P.O. Box 141000, Nashville, Tennessee 37214.

Rutledge Hill Press books may be purchased in bulk for educational, business, fundraising, or sales promotional use. For information, please e-mail SpecialMarkets@ThomasNelson.com.

Library of Congress Cataloging-in-Publication Data

Foxworthy, Jeff.

    No redneck left behind : facing the real world after gettin' your diploma / Jeff Foxworthy; with illustrations by David Boyd.

    p. cm.

    ISBN 1-4016-0231-2

    1. Rednecks—Humor. 2. Education—Humor. 3. Work—Humor. I. Title.

PN6231.R38F6748 2006

818' .5402—dc22   2005032398

Printed in the United States of America

06 07 08 09 10 — 5 4 3 2 1

Introduction

The first person in my extended family who ever bragged about his education claimed to be a "graduate of the school of hard knocks." That meant his wife had hit him upside the head with a ball bat enough times that he knew better than to come home drunk at three in the morning.

When we had our first high school graduate, no one in the family would speak to him for six months because, they said, "He thinks he's better'n the rest of us." He never said that, of course, but he did keep the graduation tassel hanging from his rear-view mirror for the rest of his life . . . right next to his Beech-Nut air freshener.

So when I entered college at Georgia Tech, I knew I was setting myself up to be ostracized (Uncle Elmer thinks that's a giant chicken that buries its head in the sand, and I'm not telling him otherwise). But my family's cold shoulder turned into a slap on the back a couple of years later when I dropped out of school to go to work for IBM. Finally I had done something they understood. When my younger brother later went to Duke University, we told the family that he was serving a four-year sentence for business administration. They were so proud.

As you can see, I know a lot about getting educated, getting a job, and getting on in life. I know that "beginner's luck" is not a legitimate job skill to include on your résumé, that wearing the clothes I slept in to work the next day isn't "dressing for success," that a high score on a cholesterol test is not a sign of intelligence, and that advice on worming hogs doesn't qualify as a stock tip. These are only a few of the lessons I've learned in life that I'm now willing to share with others.

I hope you enjoy *No Redneck Left Behind* and come to understand that it has nothing to do with mooning.

—Jeff Foxworthy

Your Ph.D. stands
for posthole digger.

You've ever been
promoted to dishwasher.

Your savings account
is the ashtray
in your truck.

The only diploma
on your wall
is from DUI school.

LATER...

You made up your
Social Security number.

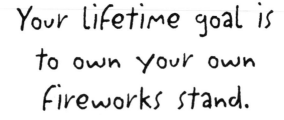

Your lifetime goal is
to own your own
fireworks stand.

You've spent more
time on parole
than on payroll.

11

You say you're
in the oil business
because you pump
gas for a living.

...AND THE BASS SINGER IN THIS YEAR'S QUARTET...

Your voice changed
in the third grade.

Your résumé includes
your high scores on
video games.

14

The only big bucks
you'll ever come into
are hanging over
your fireplace.

15

Your class voted you
"Most likely to return fire."

You make a car payment on time and the bank calls to see if you're okay.

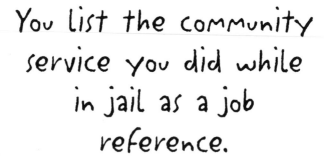

You list the community service you did while in jail as a job reference.

18

Your idea of
a Palm Pilot is writing
notes to yourself
on your hand.

19

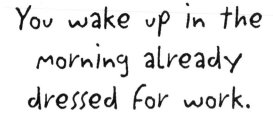

You wake up in the
morning already
dressed for work.

You've ever studied
for a rectal exam.

You call your
boss "dude."

Your keepsake from prom night came nine months later and weighed seven pounds, three ounces.

You've ever told a bill collector you were dead.

The only
newspapers you
read are sold in
the checkout line of
the grocery store.

LATER...

You have a tattoo that says "Born to bag groceries."

26

The stock market crashes and it doesn't affect you one bit.

27

Your business
mailing address is
c/o Waffle House.

28

Your mama ever
started a fistfight at a high
school sports event.

29

You were ever fired
for shooting spitballs.

Your retirement plans include getting your own place.

You carry a case of beer
to your tax audit.

Three generations
of your family are
currently working at
McDonald's.

You won't work on
Garth's birthday.

34

Your "Arizona State" shirt is from the penitentiary, not the university.

35

Your taxidermist also
does your taxes.

36

You played banjo in the high
school marching band.

You've held
a business lunch
at a vending machine.

Recycling aluminum
cans is mentioned on
your tax return.

39

Your financial planner told you
to buy lottery tickets.

40

You've ever
beaten up someone
because they had
a library card.

You think the ability to hold on to a job is overrated.

42

Your father
encourages you
to quit school because
Larry has an opening
on the lube rack.

43

Your homecoming queen had her
boyfriend's name carved on her arm.

You always make
the minimum payment
and the maximum
withdrawal.

You work without your
shirt on and so does
your husband.

46

You've ever written your résumé on a cocktail napkin.

47

You don't think reading should be a requirement for high school graduation.

Your primary source of income
is a pool stick.

You consider turkey calling a second language.

Every time you walk into the bank, the loan manager starts shaking his head "no."

51

Your high school graduation was the headline of the local paper.

THE POACHERS

You spend 40 hours
a week at Wal-Mart
but don't work there.

You think a stock
tip is advice on wormin'
your hogs.

Your mother thinks you should have been a surgeon because of the ease and confidence you have with the deep-fat fryer.

55

The ATM starts laughing when you walk up to it.

Your family business folded when
your daddy's ladder broke.

You list "beginner's luck" as a skill on a job application.

You park in handicapped
spaces based on your
SAT score.

59

You were the captain
of your high school burping team.

Your late fees
at the video store
are more than your
monthly income.

You quit your job because deer season's fixin' to start.

62

You've asked a hairstylist for a "business at the front, party at the back" cut.

63

Your medical plan is
not to get sick.

You paid for your first business
lunch with pennies.

The biggest sign on your place of business says "Minnows."

66

Your tax return consists
of "welfare in" and
"child support out."

67

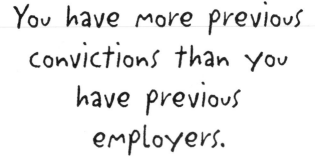

You have more previous
convictions than you
have previous
employers.

68

You were ever expelled from
school for an obscene T-shirt.

Your highest-ever
test score was for
cholesterol.

The only thing your credit card is good for is scraping frost off your windshield.

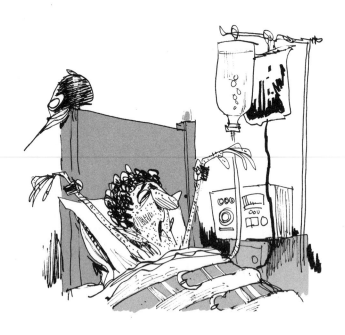

You've ever missed work because
of chigger bites.

You think
the NASDAQ 400
is a stock car race.

You list dogs as dependents on your tax form.

You've ever conducted business while sitting on the toilet.

75

Your biggest business
worry is law
enforcement.

You've shared a spit cup with your
high school sweetheart.

You're receiving disability payments as the result of a mechanical bull accident.

Your watchband is
wider than any book
you've ever read.

79

Your class reunion
is a keg party
in the woods.

LATER...

The family business
requires a lookout.

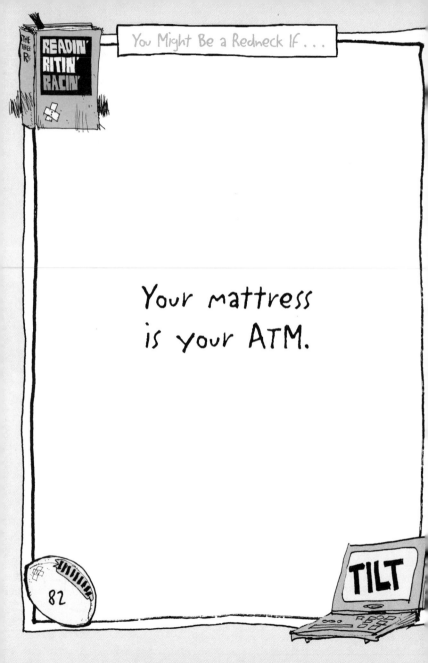

Your mattress
is your ATM.

82

You and your truant
officer shoot pool
during school hours.

You were wearing a trucker's hat
in your senior picture.

THE POACHERS

The major decisions in your life were made with the help of a Magic 8 Ball.

You list tick removal as a skill on your résumé.

86

Your college graduation
ceremony included
parallel parking
an 18-wheeler.

87

You've ever been fired from a construction job because of appearance.

You work
at the 99-Cent Store
for the employee
discount.

89

You missed sex
education class because
your baby was sick.

You answer all phone calls with "Check's in the mail."

91

Bass Pro Shop is forced
to garnish your
paycheck.

Your high school annual
is now a mug shot book
for the police department.

Every car you own has a Papa John's sign on the roof.

94